The Baby

A Division of The McGraw·Hill Companies

Columbus, Ohio

www.sra4kids.com

SRA/McGraw-Hill

A Division of The **McGraw·Hill** *Companies*

Printed in the United States of America.

Send all inquiries to:
SRA/McGraw-Hill
8787 Orion Place
Columbus, OH 43240-4027

ISBN 0-07-569409-3
   3 4 5 6 7 8 9 DBH 05 04 03 02

The Cake

The  is in the ⬜ .

baby   chair

The  is on the .

cake

ear

The  is on the .

cake   nose

The  is on the .

cake · hands

The  is on the  .

cake

girl

The  is in the ▢ .

girl   tub

The ▢ is in the ▢ .

baby   tub

9

The Shirt

The  is on the .

shirt   head

The  are on the .

pants   arms

The  are on the .

socks   hands

The  is on the .

shirt   arms

The  are on the .

pants   legs

The  are on the .

socks   feet